What Am I?

By

LINDA GRANFIELD

Illustrated by

JENNIFER HERBERT

Tundra Books

Text copyright © 2007 by Linda Granfield

Illustrations copyright © 2007 by Jennifer Herbert

Published in Canada by Tundra Books,

75 Sherbourne Street, Toronto, Ontario M5A 2P9

Published in the United States by Tundra Books of Northern New York,

P.O. Box 1030, Plattsburgh, New York 12901

Library of Congress Control Number: 2006909133

Library and Archives Canada Cataloguing in Publication

Granfield, Linda
         What Am I? / Linda Granfield ; illustrated by Jennifer Herbert.

ISBN 978-0-88776-812-5
         1. Riddles, Juvenile.   2. Guessing games – Juvenile literature.
I. Herbert, Jennifer II. Title.

GV1473.G73 2007   j793.735   C2006-905779-6

We acknowledge the financial support of the Government of Canada through the
Book Publishing Industry Development Program (BPIDP) and that of the Government of Ontario
through the Ontario Media Development Corporation's Ontario Book Initiative. We further
acknowledge the support of the Canada Council for the Arts and the Ontario Arts Council
for our publishing program.

ONTARIO ARTS COUNCIL
CONSEIL DES ARTS DE L'ONTARIO

The illustrations for this book were rendered in gouache on Arches paper

Design: Terri Nimmo

Printed and bound in Canada

3 4 5 6   16

In memory of
Brian Alexander Granfield – 1960-1961.

L.G.

For Max, my little man with all the questions.
Here are some answers.

J.H.

What am I?

I have wheels.

I can take you far.

I have pedals you must push.

Can you guess?

A wagon?

A bicycle?

A shopping cart?

A baby stroller?

A toy truck?

I am a bicycle.

I have two wheels.
You can ride me around the block
or in races around the world.
I am a good way to exercise
while you travel.

What am I?

I fit in a pocket.
I can beep and play songs.
I am helpful in an emergency.

Can you guess?

A keyring?
A wallet?
A cell phone?
A radio?
A whistle?

I am a cell phone.

I can show you who is calling.
Sometimes I take pictures, too.
I can be quiet and still let you
know someone wants to talk to you.

What am I?

I am round.
I have a hole in the middle.
I am fried and I'm sweet.

Can you guess?

A bagel?
A candy?
A ball of twine?
A doughnut?
A vase?

I am a doughnut.

I am made of flour, sugar, yeast, and fat. Sometimes, I have colored sprinkles all over me. You can eat the doughnut "holes," too!

What am I?

I am sharp.
I come in a pair.
I can be used outside in winter
and inside in summer.

Can you guess?

Scissors?
Ice skates?
A sled?
A skateboard?
Skis?

I am ice skates.

I'm worn by people of all ages.
I am used on backyard rinks
and at the Olympic Games.
Long laces help keep me
on your feet.

What am I?

I can be worn or
carried by you.
I go to school and camp.
I need to be cleaned out
once in a while.

Can you guess?

A suitcase?
A cardboard box?
A plastic bag?
A backpack?
A basket?

I am a backpack.

I have lots of pockets.

I help you carry many things.

I keep your books and papers dry.

What am I?

I can fly with big wings.
I take off and land.
I take people to work and play.

Can you guess?

An owl?
A bat?
An airplane?
A bee?
A train?

I am an airplane.

I can carry one person
or hundreds of people,
depending on my size.
The airport is my home.
I fly high above the clouds.

What am I?

I am very small.
I am found where it's cold.
I have six points.

Can you guess?

An ice-cream cone?
A polar bear?
A snowflake?
An ice cube?
An icicle?

I am a snowflake.

I can stick to your eyelashes.
I am made of frozen water.
I help you make snowmen
and snowballs.